Healthy Keto Smoothies

Easy and Delicious Ketogenic Smoothies Recipes to Lose Weight, Gain Energy and Feel Great in Your Body

Dr Mark Hogan

Table of contents

INTRODUCTION

If you are on a Ketogenic Diet and are looking for a quick and easy way to satisfy your craving, then Smoothies are the perfect snack to go for!

They are not only healthy and fulfilling but will help you to stay on your Ketosis while filling up that food itch you have.

They are easy to make and take minimal time and effort, even though the advantages are immense!

Since everything is in liquid form, the body absorbs all the essential macronutrients very quickly and helps your body to follow and adjust itself to the Ketogenic diet with ease.

I have tried my very best to make this book as accessible and easy to understand and as possible! In doing so, I have included two pretty detailed intro chapters covering the basics of the Ketogenic Diet and Keto Smoothies.

This is followed by a plethora of amazing Keto Smoothie recipes that you are sure to enjoy!

I bid you a happy and healthy life!

CHAPTER 1: THE FUNDAMENTALS OF KETO

Losing weight is a huge challenge for almost anyone! But when you add in the fact that you have a hectic schedule, things become much more complicated!

You never get enough time to go to a gym or engage in enough physical activities that would help your weight loss.

Following a strict diet might be challenging in times like these, but that doesn't mean that we have to let go of our dreams of having a healthy physique right?

This is where the Ketogenic Diet and Smoothies come in!

What is the Ketogenic Diet?

So, before moving forward, let me explain a little bit about Ketogenic Diet first.

Well, we all know that our body requires energy for the proper functioning of our cells and organs right? And for getting this energy, the body uses carbohydrates as the most common source of energy.

However, because we have been exposing ourselves to high carb and a low-fat diet for so long, we have become used to depending on glucose (coming from carbohydrates) as the main source of energy.

As long as glucose is in our body, the body will opt to use glucose as the primary source of energy. It is only when the carb level goes down, that our body starts to look for other sources energy, which is fat!

The main point then? If you eventually cut down the carbohydrate intake of your body, then your body will turn into a fat burning machine through the method of Ketosis.

So, the next point to know about is Ketosis-

Having a look at Ketosis

Once your body decides that it is time to start burning fat, the body takes the fat to the liver where it is broken down into glycerol and fatty acids through a process known as Beta-Oxidation.

These fatty acids are broken down to even further smaller molecules through a process of Ketogenesis, which leads to the creation of a very specific ketone known as acetoacetate.

Given enough time, the body slowly starts to completely adapt itself to use these ketones as a source of energy, and the muscles learn to convert the acetoacetate into Beta-Hydroxybutyrate (BHB for short), which is the body's preferred Ketogenic source of energy for the brain.

Asides from that, acetone is also produced, which the body expels as waste.

The glycerol created during the beta-oxidation goes through a process known as gluconeogenesis that converts the glycerol into glucose that the body uses for energy.

Alternatively, the excess protein obtained during a Keto diet is also utilized for energy by converting them to Glucose.

This allows the body to satisfy the minimum need for Glucose of the body without actually using carbohydrates to get it!

Symptoms of being in Ketosis

Now that you are a little bit familiar with Ketosis, the following are the signs are symptoms that you should look out for to ensure that you are in Ketosis.

- Your mouth will feel dry, and you feel have increased thirst
- The number of washroom visits will increase as you might need to urinate more often.
- Your breath will have a slight "Fruity" smell to it that will resemble that of a nail polish
- Aside from those three, you will get the sensation mentioned above of having a low hunger level and increased natural energy.

Some adverse effects to know about

While on a Ketogenic Diet, your body will undergo a lot of different changes as it tries to adapt to the new diet. Therefore, you might experience some uncomfortable feelings, however, rest assured that they will go away within a week or two.

- Dizziness
- Aggravation
- Headaches
- Keto-Flu
- Mental Fogginess

Aside from those, some symptoms which you should be aware of are:

- **Frequent desire to urinate:** Since Ketosis will cause your body to burn up more fat, the glycogen gets stored up. In this situation, your Kidneys will start to process a lot of water and excrete them, increasing your desire to urinate.

- **Hypoglycemia:** This means that your sugar level might lower down

- **Constipation:** This is yet another effect that you should keep in mind and it primarily occurs due to dehydration and lower salt intake. This can be tackled very easily by drinking more water.

- **Increased Sugar Craving:** The early start of your diet might give you a severe craving for sugar! This can be tackled by increasing your protein and Vitamin B complex intake. Asides from that, you can go for some morning walks as well.

- **Diarrhea:** This is a standard issue which is faced by some people during the first few days, but it resolves itself automatically after a few days.

- **Sleep problem:** This might be a result of the reduced levels of serotonin or insulin.

Once your body is in Ketosis, it will start to flush out electrolytes from the body, and this is one of the main reasons as to why the above-mentioned symptoms take place.

This diuretic effect can be tackled very easily by drinking more and more water and slightly increasing your salt intake.

Ingredients to consider for your Keto Smoothies and other meals

Fats: Try to take more saturated and Monosaturated varieties of fat.

- Saturated fats include lard, tallow, duck fat, chicken fat, ghee, etc.
- Monounsaturated fats include avocado oil, olive oil, and macadamia oil
- Fats rich in poly-saturated Omega-3s extracted from animal sources
- Cocoa butter, coconut butter

- 90% or higher dark chocolate
- Palm shortening
- Chia seeds

Vegetables: When choosing your vegetable, try to avoid root vegetables and stick to the green leafy ones as they will help you to keep your carbohydrates level at a minimum.

- Watercress
- Zucchini
- Spinach
- Tomatoes
- Shallots
- Seaweeds
- Pumpkin
- Scallions
- Radishes
- Okra
- Onions
- Mushrooms
- All leafy greens
- Lettuce
- Garlic
- Fennel
- Cucumber
- Chives
- Cauliflower
- Chives

- Celery

- Carrots

- Cabbage

- Broccoli

- Bell Pepper

- Asparagus

- Artichokes

Fruits: Regarding a Ketogenic diet, most fruits are off the table, mainly because of the high level of fructose. However, small amounts of berries are allowed.

Good choices for fruits are:

- Avocado

- Olives

- Blackberry

- Lime

- Lemon

- Blueberry

- Raspberry

- Strawberry

- Cranberry

Legumes: Similar to fruits, all types of legumes are off the table. However, a minimal amount of peas or green beans can be included in your diet.

Dairy Products: In general, the following dairy products are right for your soul

- Kefir

- Full fat yogurt
- Full fat raw cheese
- Full fat cottage cheese
- Heavy whipping cream
- Full fat sour cream
- Full fat cream cheese
- Ghee
- Butter

Drinks: All types of sweet or aerated drinks are to be avoided entirely in your Keto diet. Drink of plenty of water though! Good drinks include:

- Coconut milk
- Almond milk
- Cashew milk
- Broth and soups
- Herbal teas
- Coffee teas
- Water
- Seltzer water
- Club soda
- Lemon and lime juices
- Sparkline water
- Water

Nuts and Seeds: In general nuts and seeds are allowed, but you should try to keep your intake at low levels since they enhance your carbohydrate intake. Be cautious while consuming nuts. However, keep in mind that you are to avoid peanuts as they fall under the legume category.

The following are allowed though:

- Almonds
- Macadamias
- Hazelnuts
- Pecans
- Pistachios
- Pine nuts
- Pumpkin seeds
- Sesame seeds
- Psyllium seeds
- Sunflower seeds
- Cashew nuts
- Walnuts
- Chia seeds

Herbs and Spices: As for herbs and spices, you are allowed to experiment with a wide variety of spices and herbs to enhance the flavor of your meals. Just make sure to avoid store-bought spices and herb that have hidden sugars of MSG's as they would break your Keto diet.

Recommended spices include:

- Black pepper
- White pepper
- Sea salt
- Basil

- Chili powder
- Curry powder
- Italian seasoning
- Cumin powder
- Oregano
- Thyme
- Sage
- Rosemary
- Turmeric
- Parsley
- Cilantro
- Cinnamon
- Cloves
- Allspices
- Paprika
- Ginger
- Cardamom

CHAPTER 2: THE FANTASTIC ADVANTAGES OF KETO DIET

Now that you have a good idea of the basics of Ketogenic Diet, the following are some of the fantastic advantages that you will enjoy in the long run!

Improved Sleep Cycle: Having an adequately implemented Ketogenic Diet will help you to get a more sound sleep. Many Keto followers have reported that they were able to sleep with ease.

Improved Digestion: It will help you to improve your digestion and improve gut health as well.

Improve mood: The production of Ketones will help you to stabilize your mood by controlling the neurotransmitters such as serotonin and dopamine.

Will keep you energized: Ketones are a much more reliable energy source for your body, and it will keep you feeling energized for the whole day. Chronic fatigue symptoms that you might be experiencing will soon go away, and you will feel more energetic.

Since you are cutting down your reliance on using carbs as a source of energy, your body will also be spared of "Sugar Rush" effect where your body gets brief surges of "energy" followed by a prolonged period of fatigue.

If your body is using Ketones as the energy source, your body will continuously stay fueled due to the abundance of fat present in your body.

It will help you fight lots of diseases: The various forms of Ketogenic Diet have been seen to defend against various diseases such as Alzheimer's, Depression, Traumatic Brain Injury, Stroke, Polycystic Ovary Syndrome and so on.

Cancer is also one of the diseases that is seen to be helped with the Ketogenic Diet.

Improved Weight Loss: Trimming down your carb intake is one of the best ways to cut down your weight, as it will turn your body into a fat burning machine!

By preventing the accumulation of sugar in your body, Ketogenic Diet drives down insulin production that forces your body to use stored fat as a source of energy.

It will help you to maintain optimal weight effortlessly: If your body is adapted to a Keto diet, it will mean that your body has turned into a mean big fat burning machine!

This means that the amount of effort that you would need put to maintain your optimal physique and body weight will be significantly reduced, as your body will keep burning fat throughout the day.

This also applies to physical activities such as exercises as well! The fat burning mode of your body will further enhance the effectiveness of your daily exercise and physical activities.

Your body will start to use fat as its fuel: This is already discussed in the previous chapter, but once your body adapts itself to the Ketogenic diet, your body will go into a state of Ketosis whereupon it will encourage it exponentially burn more fat.

It helps to regulate insulin levels: Insulin is needed by our bodies as it facilitates the blood sugar levels. Insulin acts as a kind of messenger between glucose and our body cells, letting it know when to start using glucose as a source of energy.

While you are on a higher carb diet, your body will essentially experience more insulin spikes every time your blood sugar level rises.

Nutritional Ketosis helps to facilitate the reduction of insulin levels because of your lower blood sugar levels through lowered consumption of carbs.

All of the above-mentioned symptoms can be easily managed by following a Ketogenic

CHAPTER 3: THE KETO MISTAKES TO AVOID

The following are some of the early mistakes that individuals tend to avoid during their early Keto days.

Losing patience: This is extremely crucial and is a deal breaker for many! You should keep in mind that a Ketogenic Diet won't bear results overnight, and it will take some time. So, don't lose your patience and prepare yourself for the journey ahead.

Not drinking enough water: Without drinking a right amount of water, your body won't be able to do what it's supposed to do correctly! You have to drink more water than you used to during a Keto diet to ensure that your whole body is working correctly. A general rule of thumb is to drink at least 0.5 to 1 ounces of water per pound of your body weight per day.

Comparing yourself to others: This is one of the biggest mistakes that individuals tend to make! You should appreciate the fact that every single individual's body reacts differently to dietary changes and some people progress faster than others. You should not feel disheartened by seeing that your friend is losing weight faster than you! Remember, slow and steady wins the race.

Not getting proper sleep: Just like water, your body requires a right amount of sleep. Otherwise it will fall into a state of fatigue, making you feel lethargic all throughout the day.

Not preparing a meal plan: Meal Planning or prepping is something that individuals often ignore, but it is essential! Those who do not make a proper meal plan, often end up failing to accurately follow the diet and end up being hungry and overeating! Therefore, a Meal Plan is crucial as it will save you from these frustrations.

CHAPTER 4: A NOTE ON MAKING THE PERFECT KETO SMOOTHIE

The Keto Smoothie Format

Smoothie making is an art that requires time and practice to master. However, if you are new to this field and want to create amazing Smoothies right away! Just follow the basic Smoothie format provided below.

It will help you create amazing Keto Smoothies in no time!

It is as follows:

> **Choose Smoothie Recipe + Add Liquid + Add Keto Fat + Add Desired Flavor+ Additional Nutrients + Desired Topping + Final Blend = Ground Breaking Smoothie Ready!**

Let me break down the components individually for you.

The Recipe

The recipe will always act as the foundation of the Smoothie that you are making. In our case, since we are trying to make Keto friendly recipes, we will choose our ingredients accordingly.

The Liquid

Once you have chosen your recipe, the next step is to add the liquid first. This allows the other ingredients from getting stuck.

Keto Smoothies should be creamy, so always try to go for high-fat options. However, refrain yourself from high sugar options such as orange juices as they will push you out of Ketosis.

In case you are experimenting, good options for liquid include:

- Coconut cream
- Unsweetened coconut milk
- Cashew nut/ seed milk
- Water
- Tea
- Coffee

The Fat

The fats will help you to keep your Smoothies creamy so, it is essential that you choose the right fat for your Smoothie.

Avocados are excellent as they will help you create a creamy texture without adding extra carbs.

Avocados are pretty much packed with Monosaturated fats and fiber that will help you kick up the effectiveness of your Keto smoothie as well.

Other good options include:

- Coconut oil
- MCT Oil
- Cashew Cream
- Coconut Cream
- Avocado Oil
- Raw Eggs
- Coconut Yogurt
- Almond Butter

The Flavors

Perhaps one of the best things about Smoothie is that you can modify them to your heart's content and add your desired flavors. In most cases, you will be following the recipes, however, if you decide you experiment, the following are good options to consider:

- Unsweetened vanilla extract
- Unsweetened cocoa powder
- Various flavor extracts (no added sugar)
- Coffee
- Blueberries, raspberries, strawberries

You may add some spices as well such as:

- Matcha
- Cinnamon
- Turmeric

Etc.

Additional Nutrients

If you want to add make your Smoothie more nutritious, the following might help you. They will make your smoothies more jam-packed and allow you to get more nutrients without hours of cooking.

Mixins may include:

- Brazilian nuts
- Greens
- Prebiotic Fiber

- Collagen Powder
- Protein Powder

Once you are done adding all the ingredients, blend it up and enjoy! But before you do that! You should try to decorate your smoothie with some additional toppings as well if you want.

Desired Toppings

These toppings will make your smoothie look both delicious and tasty!

- Unsweetened coconut flakes
- Cacao Nibs
- Berries
- Chopped nuts
- Poppy seeds

Common Smoothie Blunders

If you are an amateur Smoothie artist, then it is very natural that you may face some difficulties early on. The following tips should help you deal with some of the most common issues:

- Too Frothy: If frothiness is the issue, try to add a little less liquid and not blend it for too long. Alternatively, you may withhold a portion of the liquid and gradually added it later on once the other half of the ingredients are properly blended. Keep in mind that when using base ingredients such as Avocado, banana, etc. you won't need much liquid as they already have a fair amount of liquid on their own.
- Too Runny: If you find your Smoothie to be too runny, lower down the amount of liquid and add more thickening ingredients.

- Not sweet enough/tasty: Add a bit of your desired natural sweetener, honey, dates or maple syrup are good options.

- Too bitter: An excellent way to tackle bitterness is to lower the number of greens and add some fruits.

- Not blending correctly: If you find that you are unable to blend your ingredients properly, try to cut them into small pieces and add them to your blender. This usually solves the problem.

CHAPTER 5: THE AMAZING KETO SMOOTHIE GALORE

Amazing Nutty Choco Milk Shake

Serving: 1

Prep Time: 10 minutes

Ingredients:

- ¼ cup whole milk
- 1 tablespoons cocoa powder
- 1 pack stevia
- 1/4 cup pecans
- 1 and ½ cups water
- 1 tablespoons macadamia oil

Directions:

1. Add listed ingredients to blender
2. Blend until you have a smooth and creamy texture
3. Serve chilled and enjoy!

Nutritional Contents:

- Calories: 358
- Fat: 34g
- Carbohydrates: 15g
- Protein: 5g

Delicious Creamy Choco Shake

Serving: 1

Prep Time: 10 minutes

Ingredients:

- ½ cup heavy cream
- 2 tablespoons cocoa powder
- 1 pack stevia
- 1 cup water

Directions:

1. Add listed ingredients to blender
2. Blend until you have a smooth and creamy texture
3. Serve chilled and enjoy!

Nutritional Contents:

- Calories: 435
- Fat: 45g
- Carbohydrates: 10g
- Protein: 5g

Mesmerizing Strawberry and Chocolate Shake

Serving: 1

Prep Time: 10 minutes

Ingredients:

- ½ cup heavy cream, liquid
- 1 tablespoons cocoa powder
- 1 pack stevia
- ½ cup strawberry, sliced
- 1 tablespoons coconut flakes, unsweetened
- 1 and ½ cups water

Directions:

1. Add listed ingredients to blender
2. Blend until you have a smooth and creamy texture
3. Serve chilled and enjoy!

Nutritional Contents:

- Calories: 470
- Fat: 46g
- Carbohydrates: 15g
- Protein: 4g

The Feisty Nut Shake

Serving: 1

Prep Time: 10 minutes

Ingredients:

- ¼ cup heavy cream, liquid
- ½ tablespoon cocoa powder
- 1 pack stevia
- ¼ cup almonds, sliced
- ¼ cup macadamia nuts, whole
- 1 tablespoon flaxseed
- 1 tablespoon hemp seed
- 1 cup water

Directions:

1. Add listed ingredients to blender
2. Blend until you have a smooth and creamy texture
3. Serve chilled and enjoy!

Nutritional Contents:

- Calories: 590
- Fat: 57g
- Carbohydrates: 17g
- Protein: 12g

The Overloaded Berry Shake

Serving: 1

Prep Time: 10 minutes

Ingredients:

- ½ cup whole milk yogurt
- 1 pack stevia
- ¼ cup raspberries
- ¼ cup blackberry
- ¼ cup strawberries, chopped
- 1 tablespoon cocoa powder
- 1 tablespoon avocado oil
- 1 and ½ cups water

Directions:

1. Add listed ingredients to blender
2. Blend until you have a smooth and creamy texture
3. Serve chilled and enjoy!

Nutritional Contents:

- Calories: 255
- Fat: 19g
- Carbohydrates: 20g
- Protein: 6g

The Fat Burner Espresso Smoothie

Serving: 2

Prep Time: 10 minutes

Ingredients:

- 1 scoop Isopure Zero Carb protein powder
- 1 espresso shot
- ¼ cup Greek yogurt, full fat
- Liquid stevia, to sweeten
- Pinch of cinnamon
- 5 ice cubes

Directions:

1. Add listed ingredients to blender
2. Blend until you have a smooth and creamy texture
3. Serve chilled and enjoy!

Nutritional Contents:

- Calories: 270
- Fat: 16g
- Carbohydrates: 2g
- Protein: 30g

The Curious Raspberry and Green Shake

Serving: 1

Prep Time: 10 minutes

Ingredients:

- 1 cup whole milk
- 1 pack stevia
- ¼ cup raspberry
- 1 cup water
- 1 tablespoons macadamia oil
- 1 cup spinach

Directions:

1. Add listed ingredients to blender
2. Blend until you have a smooth and creamy texture
3. Serve chilled and enjoy!

Nutritional Contents:

- Calories: 292
- Fat: 21g
- Carbohydrates: 17g
- Protein: 9g

The Great Shamrock Shake

Serving: 1

Prep Time: 10 minutes

Ingredients:

- 1 cup coconut milk, unsweetened
- 1 avocado, peeled, pitted and sliced
- liquid stevia
- 1 cup ice
- 1 tablespoon pure vanilla extract
- 1 teaspoon pure peppermint extract

Directions:

1. Add listed ingredients to blender
2. Blend until you have a smooth and creamy texture
3. Serve chilled and enjoy!

Nutritional Contents:

- Calories: 195
- Fat: 19g
- Carbohydrates: 4.4g
- Protein: 2g

The Strawberry Almond Smoothie

Serving: 1

Prep Time: 10 minutes

Ingredients:

- 16 ounces unsweetened almond milk, vanilla
- 1 pack stevia
- 4 ounces heavy cream
- 1 scoop vanilla whey protein
- ¼ cup frozen strawberries, unsweetened

Directions:

1. Add all the listed ingredients to a blender.
2. Blend on high until smooth and creamy.
3. Enjoy your smoothie.

Nutritional Contents:

- Calories: 304
- Fat: 25g
- Carbohydrates: 7g
- Protein: 15g

Early Morning Fruit Smoothie

Serving: 1

Prep Time: 10 minutes

Ingredients:

- 1 cup Spring mix salad blend
- 2 cups water
- 3 medium blackberries, whole
- 1 packet Stevia, optional
- 1 tablespoon avocado oil
- 1 tablespoon coconut flakes shredded and unsweetened
- 2 tablespoons pecans, chopped
- 1 tablespoon hemp seed
- 1 tablespoon sunflower seed

Directions:

1. Add all the listed ingredients to a blender.
2. Blend on high until smooth and creamy.
3. Enjoy your smoothie.

Nutritional Contents:

- Calories: 385
- Fat: 34g
- Carbohydrates: 16g
- Protein: 6.9g

Hazelnut and Coconut Medley

Serving: 1

Prep Time: 10 minutes

Ingredients:

- ½ cup coconut milk
- ¼ cup hazelnuts, chopped
- 1 and ½ cups water
- 1 pack stevia

Directions:

1. Add listed ingredients to blender
2. Blend until you have a smooth and creamy texture
3. Serve chilled and enjoy!

Nutritional Contents:

- Calories: 457
- Fat: 46g
- Carbohydrates: 12g
- Protein: 7g

The Green Minty Smoothie

Serving: 1

Prep Time: 10 minutes

Ingredients:

- 1 stalk celery
- 2 cups water
- 2 ounces almonds
- 1 packet Stevia
- 1 cup spinach
- 2 mint leaves

Directions:

1. Add listed ingredients to blender
2. Blend until you have a smooth and creamy texture
3. Serve chilled and enjoy!

Nutritional Contents:

- Calories: 417
- Fat: 43g
- Carbohydrates: 10g
- Protein: 5.5g

Cucumber Spinach Smoothie

Serving: 1

Prep Time: 10 minutes

Ingredients:

- 2 large handful spinach
- ½ cucumber, peeled and cubed
- 6 ice cubes
- 1 cup coconut milk
- Liquid stevia, to sweeten
- ½ teaspoon xanthan gum
- 1-2 tablespoons MCT oil

Directions:

1. Add listed ingredients to blender
2. Blend until you have a smooth and creamy texture
3. Serve chilled and enjoy!

Nutritional Contents:

- Calories: 335
- Fat: 33g
- Carbohydrates: 4g
- Protein: 3g

Overloaded Hazelnut and Mocha Shake

Serving: 1

Prep Time: 10 minutes

Ingredients:

- 2 tablespoons cocoa powder
- 2 cups brewed coffee, chilled
- 1 tablespoon MCT oil
- 1-2 packet Stevia, optional
- 1 ounce Hazelnuts

Directions:

1. Add all the listed ingredients to a blender.
2. Blend on high until smooth and creamy.
3. Enjoy your smoothie.

Nutritional Contents:

- Calories: 325
- Fat: 33g
- Carbohydrates: 12g
- Protein: 6.8g

The Great Avocado and Almond Delight

Serving: 1

Prep Time: 10 minutes

Ingredients:

- ½ cup unsweetened almond milk, vanilla
- ½ cup half and half
- ½ avocado, peeled, pitted and sliced
- 1 tablespoon almond butter
- 1 scoop zero carb protein powder
- Pinch of cinnamon
- ½ teaspoon vanilla extract
- 2-4 ice cubes
- Liquid stevia

Directions:

1. Add all the listed ingredients to a blender.
2. Blend on high until smooth and creamy.
3. Enjoy your smoothie.

Nutritional Contents:

- Calories: 252
- Fat: 18g
- Carbohydrates: 5g
- Protein: 17g

Simple Vanilla Hemp

Serving: 1

Prep Time: 10 minutes

Ingredients:

- 1 cup water
- 1 cup unsweetened hemp milk, vanilla
- 1 and ½ tablespoons coconut oil, unrefined
- ½ cup frozen blueberries, mixed
- 4 cup leafy greens, kale and spinach
- 1 tablespoons flaxseeds
- 1 tablespoons almond butter

Directions:

1. Add listed ingredients to blender
2. Blend until you have a smooth and creamy texture
3. Serve chilled and enjoy!

Nutritional Contents:

- Calories: 250
- Fat: 20g
- Carbohydrates: 10g
- Protein: 7g

Subtle Raspberry Smoothie

Serving: 1

Prep Time: 10 minutes

Ingredients:

- ½ cup raspberries
- 1 cup unsweetened almond milk, vanilla
- 1 scoop prebiotic fiber
- 1 scoop vanilla whey protein powder
- 2 tablespoons coconut oil
- ¼ cup coconut flakes, unsweetened
- 3-4 ice cubes

Directions:

1. Add all the listed ingredients to a blender.
2. Blend on high until smooth and creamy.
3. Enjoy your smoothie.

Nutritional Contents:

- Calories: 258
- Fat: 22g
- Carbohydrates: 7g
- Protein: 14g

The Nutty Macadamia Delight

Serving: 1

Prep Time: 10 minutes

Ingredients:

- 1 tablespoon chia seeds
- 1 cup spinach
- Oz Macadamia nuts
- 1 packet stevia, if you want
- 2/3 cup water
- ¼ cup heavy cream

Directions:

1. Add listed ingredients to blender
2. Blend until you have a smooth and creamy texture
3. Serve chilled and enjoy!

Nutritional Contents:

- Calories: 485
- Fat: 48g
- Carbohydrates: 13g
- Protein: 7g

The Ultimate Mocha Milk Shake

Serving: 1

Prep Time: 10 minutes

Ingredients:

- 1 cup whole milk
- 2 tablespoons cocoa powder
- 2 pack stevia
- 1 cup brewed coffee, chilled
- 1 tablespoon coconut oil

Directions:

1. Add listed ingredients to blender
2. Blend until you have a smooth and creamy texture
3. Serve chilled and enjoy!

Nutritional Contents:

- Calories: 293
- Fat: 23g
- Carbohydrates: 19g
- Protein: 10g

A Kale and Spinach Glass

Serving: 2

Prep Time: 10 minutes

Ingredients:

- Handful of kale
- Handful of spinach
- 2 broccoli heads
- 1 tomato
- Handful of lettuce
- 1 avocado, cubed
- 1 cucumber, cubed
- Juice of ½ lemon
- Pineapple juice as needed

Directions:

1. Add listed ingredients to blender
2. Blend until you have a smooth and creamy texture
3. Serve chilled and enjoy!

Nutritional Contents:

- Calories: 157
- Fat: 18g
- Carbohydrates: 10g

- Protein: 2g

A Mean Green Milk Shake

Serving: 1

Prep Time: 10 minutes

Ingredients:

- 1 cup whole milk
- 1 pack stevia
- 1 tablespoon coconut flakes, unsweetened
- 1 cup water
- 2 cups spring mix salad
- 1 tablespoons coconut oil

Directions:

1. Add listed ingredients to blender
2. Blend until you have a smooth and creamy texture
3. Serve chilled and enjoy!

Nutritional Contents:

- Calories: 309
- Fat: 23g
- Carbohydrates: 18g
- Protein: 9.5g

Very Creamy Green Machine

Serving: 1

Prep Time: 10 minutes

Ingredients:

- ½ cup unsweetened almond milk, vanilla
- ½ cup half and half
- ½ avocado, peeled, pitted and sliced
- ½ cup frozen blueberries, unsweetened
- 1 cup spinach
- 1 tablespoon almond butter
- 1 scoop Zero Carb protein powder
- 2-4 ice cubes
- 1 pack stevia

Directions:

1. Add listed ingredients to blender
2. Blend until you have a smooth and creamy texture
3. Serve chilled and enjoy!

Nutritional Contents:

- Calories: 279
- Fat: 18g
- Carbohydrates: 9g

- Protein: 18g

The Healthy Yogurt and Kale Delight

Serving: 1

Prep Time: 10 minutes

Ingredients:

- 1 cup whole milk yogurt
- 1 cup baby kale greens
- 1 pack stevia
- 1 tablespoon MCT oil
- 1 tablespoons sunflower seeds
- 1 cup water

Directions:

1. Add listed ingredients to blender
2. Blend until you have a smooth and creamy texture
3. Serve chilled and enjoy!

Nutritional Contents:

- Calories: 329
- Fat: 26g
- Carbohydrates: 15g
- Protein: 11g

The Sunny Side Up

Serving: 2

Prep Time: 10 minutes

Ingredients:

- 2 cups fresh spinach
- 1 and ½ cups almond milk
- ½ cup coconut water
- 2 tablespoons coconut unsweetened flakes

Directions:

1. Add listed ingredients to blender
2. Blend until you have a smooth and creamy texture
3. Serve chilled and enjoy!

Nutritional Contents:

- Calories: 485
- Fat: 38g
- Carbohydrates: 14g
- Protein: 16g

Garden Variety Green and Yogurt Delight

Serving: 1

Prep Time: 10 minutes

Ingredients:

- 1 cup whole milk yogurt
- 1 cup garden greens
- 1 pack stevia
- 1 tablespoon MCT oil
- 1 tablespoon flaxseed, ground
- 1 cup water

Directions:

1. Add listed ingredients to blender
2. Blend until you have a smooth and creamy texture
3. Serve chilled and enjoy!

Nutritional Contents:

- Calories: 334
- Fat: 26g
- Carbohydrates: 14g
- Protein: 11g

Magical Blueberry and Kale Mix

Serving: 1

Prep Time: 10 minutes

Ingredients:

- ½ cup whole milk yogurt
- 1 cup baby kale greens
- 1 pack stevia
- 1 tablespoons MCT oil
- ¼ cup blueberries
- 1 tablespoon pepitas
- 1 tablespoon flaxseed, ground
- 1 and ½ cups water

Directions:

1. Add listed ingredients to blender
2. Blend until you have a smooth and creamy texture
3. Serve chilled and enjoy!

Nutritional Contents:

- Calories: 307
- Fat: 24g
- Carbohydrates: 14g
- Protein: 9g

Subtle Strawberry and Spinach Delight

Serving: 1

Prep Time: 10 minutes

Ingredients:

- ½ cup whole milk yogurt
- 1 cup spinach
- 1 pack stevia
- 1 tablespoon MCT oil
- ½ cup strawberries, chopped
- 1 tablespoons hemp seed
- 1 tablespoon flaxseed, ground
- 1 and ½ cups water

Directions:

1. Add listed ingredients to blender
2. Blend until you have a smooth and creamy texture
3. Serve chilled and enjoy!

Nutritional Contents:

- Calories: 334
- Fat: 26g
- Carbohydrates: 14g
- Protein: 10g

The Coolest 5 Lettuce Green Shake

Serving: 1

Prep Time: 10 minutes

Ingredients:

- ¾ cup whole milk yogurt
- 2 cups 5 – lettuce mix salad greens
- 1 pack stevia
- 1 tablespoon MCT oil
- 1 tablespoon chia seeds
- 1 and ½ cups water

Directions:

1. Add listed ingredients to blender
2. Blend until you have a smooth and creamy texture
3. Serve chilled and enjoy!

Nutritional Contents:

- Calories: 320
- Fat: 24g
- Carbohydrates: 17g
- Protein: 10g

Rosemary and Lemon Garden Smoothie

Serving: 1

Prep Time: 10 minutes

Ingredients:

- ½ cup whole milk yogurt
- 1 cup Garden greens
- 1 pack stevia
- 1 tablespoon olive oil
- 1 stalk fresh rosemary
- 1 tablespoon lemon juice, fresh
- 1 tablespoon pepitas
- 1 tablespoon flaxseed, ground
- 1 and ½ cups water

Directions:

1. Add listed ingredients to blender
2. Blend until you have a smooth and creamy texture
3. Serve chilled and enjoy!

Nutritional Contents:

- Calories: 312
- Fat: 25g
- Carbohydrates: 14g

- Protein: 9g

The Nutty Smoothie

Serving: 1

Prep Time: 10 minutes

Ingredients:

- 1 tablespoon chia seeds
- 2 cups water
- 1 ounces Macadamia Nuts
- 1-2 packets Stevia, optional
- 1 ounces Hazelnut

Directions:

1. Add all the listed ingredients to a blender.
2. Blend on high until smooth and creamy.
3. Enjoy your smoothie.

Nutritional Contents:

- Calories: 452
- Fat: 43g
- Carbohydrates: 15g
- Protein: 9g

The Blueberry and Chocolate Delight

Serving: 1

Prep Time: 10 minutes

Ingredients:

- ½ cup whole milk yogurt
- ¼ cup blackberries
- 1 pack stevia
- 1 tablespoon MCT oil
- 1 tablespoon Dutch Processed Cocoa Powder
- 2 tablespoons Macadamia nuts, chopped
- 1 and ½ cups water

Directions:

1. Add listed ingredients to blender
2. Blend until you have a smooth and creamy texture
3. Serve chilled and enjoy!

Nutritional Contents:

- Calories: 463
- Fat: 43g
- Carbohydrates: 17g
- Protein: 9g

The Gritty Coffee Shake

Serving: 1

Prep Time: 10 minutes

Ingredients:

- 1 tablespoon chia seeds
- 2 cups stongly brewed coffee, chilled
- 1 ounce Macadamia Nuts
- 1-2 packets Stevia, optional
- 1 tablespoon MCT oil

Directions:

1. Add all the listed ingredients to a blender.
2. Blend on high until smooth and creamy.
3. Enjoy your smoothie.

Nutritional Contents:

- Calories: 395
- Fat: 39g
- Carbohydrates: 11g
- Protein: 5.2g

The Dashing Coconut and Melon

Serving: 1

Prep Time: 10 minutes

Ingredients:

- ¼ cup whole milk yogurt
- 1 pack stevia
- 1 tablespoon coconut oil
- ½ cup melon, sliced
- 1 tablespoon coconut flakes, unsweetened
- 1 tablespoon chia seeds
- 1 and ½ cups water

Directions:

1. Add listed ingredients to blender
2. Blend until you have a smooth and creamy texture
3. Serve chilled and enjoy!

Nutritional Contents:

- Calories: 278
- Fat: 21g
- Carbohydrates: 15g
- Protein: 6g

Sensational Strawberry Medley

Serving: 2

Prep Time: 10 minutes

Ingredients:

- 1-2 handful baby greens
- 3 medium kale leaves
- 5-8 mint leaves
- 1 inch piece ginger , peeled
- 1 avocado
- 1 cup strawberries
- 6-8 ounces coconut water + 6-8 ounces filtered water
- Fresh juice of one lime
- 1-2 teaspoon olive oil

Directions:

1. Add listed ingredients to blender
2. Blend until you have a smooth and creamy texture
3. Serve chilled and enjoy!

Nutritional Contents:

- Calories: 476
- Fat: 37g
- Carbohydrates: 15g

- Protein: 16g

Healthy Raspberry and Coconut Glass

Serving: 1

Prep Time: 10 minutes

Ingredients:

- ½ cup coconut milk
- ¼ cup raspberries
- 1 cup 50/50 salad mix
- 1 pack stevia
- 1 and ½ cups water
- 1 tablespoon pepitas
- 1 tablespoon coconut oil

Directions:

1. Add listed ingredients to blender
2. Blend until you have a smooth and creamy texture
3. Serve chilled and enjoy!

Nutritional Contents:

- Calories: 408
- Fat: 41g
- Carbohydrates: 10g
- Protein: 5g

The Blueberry Bliss

Serving: 1

Prep Time: 10 minutes

Ingredients:

- 16 ounces unsweetened almond milk, vanilla
- 1 pack stevia
- 4 ounces heavy cream
- 1 scoop vanilla whey protein
- ¼ cup frozen blueberries, unsweetened

Directions:

1. Add listed ingredients to blender
2. Blend until you have a smooth and creamy texture
3. Serve chilled and enjoy!

Nutritional Contents:

- Calories: 302
- Fat: 25g
- Carbohydrates: 4g
- Protein: 15g

The Strawberry Ginger Shake

Serving: 1

Prep Time: 10 minutes

Ingredients:

- 1 cup coconut milk
- ½ teaspoon ginger powder
- 1 small stalk celery
- 1 cup spring salad mix
- 1 teaspoon sesame seeds
- 1 cup water
- 1 pack stevia

Directions:

1. Add listed ingredients to blender
2. Blend until you have a smooth and creamy texture
3. Serve chilled and enjoy!

Nutritional Contents:

- Calories: 475
- Fat: 50g
- Carbohydrates: 10g
- Protein: 7g

The Fully Supreme Avocado Smoothie

Serving: 2

Prep Time: 10 minutes

Ingredients:

- ½ avocado, cubed
- 1 cup coconut milk
- Half a lemon
- ¼ cup fresh spinach leaves
- 1 pear
- 1 tablespoon hemp. Seed powder

Toppings

- Handful of macadamia nuts
- Handful of grapes
- 2 lemon slices

Directions:

1. Add all the listed ingredients to your blender except coconut oil, salt and chili powder
2. Blend until smooth
3. Add salt, coconut oil and chili powder
4. Stir well and serve chilled!

Nutritional Contents:

- Calories: 438

- Fat: 42g
- Carbohydrates: 11g
- Protein: 5g

Cool Coco-Loco Cream Shake

Serving: 1

Prep Time: 10 minutes

Ingredients:

- ½ cup coconut milk
- 2 tablespoons Dutch processed cocoa powder, unsweetened
- 1 cup brewed coffee, chilled
- 1-2 packs stevia
- 1 tablespoon hemp seed

Directions:

1. Add listed ingredients to blender
2. Blend until you have a smooth and creamy texture
3. Serve chilled and enjoy!

Nutritional Contents:

- Calories: 354
- Fat: 34g
- Carbohydrates: 16g
- Protein: 6g

The Great Green Anti-Oxidant Delight

Serving: 2

Prep Time: 10 minutes

Ingredients:

- 1 whole ripe avocado
- 4 cups organic baby spinach leaves
- 1 cup filtered water
- Juice of 1 lemon
- 1 English cucumber, chopped
- 3 stems fresh parsley
- 5 stems fresh mint
- 1 inch piece fresh ginger
- 2 large ice cubes

Directions:

1. Add listed ingredients to blender
2. Blend until you have a smooth and creamy texture
3. Serve chilled and enjoy!

Nutritional Contents:

- Calories: 485
- Fat: 38g
- Carbohydrates: 18g
- Protein: 16g

Cayenne Spices Chocolate Shake

Serving: 1

Prep Time: 10 minutes

Ingredients:

- ¼ cup coconut cream
- 2 tablespoons unrefined coconut oil
- 1 tablespoon whole chia seeds
- 2 tablespoons cacao
- Dash of vanilla extract
- ½ pinch cayenne powder
- ½-1 cup water
- Ice cubes as needed

Directions:

1. Add listed ingredients to blender
2. Blend until you have a smooth and creamy texture
3. Serve chilled and enjoy!

Nutritional Contents:

- Calories: 258
- Fat: 26g
- Carbohydrates: 3g
- Protein: 3g

The Cacao Super Smoothie

Serving: 1

Prep Time: 10 minutes

Ingredients:

- ½ cup unsweetened almond milk, vanilla
- ½ cup half and half
- ½ avocado, peeled ,pitted, sliced
- ½ cup frozen blueberries, unsweetened
- 1 tablespoon cacao powder
- 1 scoop whey vanilla protein powder
- Liquid stevia

Directions:

1. Add listed ingredients to blender
2. Blend until you have a smooth and creamy texture
3. Serve chilled and enjoy!

Nutritional Contents:

- Calories: 445
- Fat: 14g
- Carbohydrates: 9g
- Protein: 16g

The Supreme Power Producer

Serving: 2

Prep Time: 10 minutes

Ingredients:

- ½ cup spinach
- 1 avocado, diced
- 1 cup coconut milk
- 1 tablespoon flax seed
- 2 nori sheets, roasted and crushed
- 1 garlic clove
- Salt to taste

Toppings

- Handful of pistachios
- 3 tablespoons bell pepper, finely chopped
- handful of parsley leaves

Directions:

1. Add listed ingredients to blender
2. Blend until you have a smooth and creamy texture
3. Serve chilled and enjoy!

Nutritional Contents:

- Calories: 200

- Fat: 12g

- Carbohydrates: 10g

- Protein: 16g

A Breakfast Egg Smoothie

Serving: 1

Prep Time: 10 minutes

Ingredients:

- ½ cup coconut milk, unsweetened
- ½ cup organic whole milk kefir, plain
- 4 tablespoons chia seeds
- 1 ounce egg substitute dry powder

Directions:

1. Add all the listed ingredients to a blender.
2. Blend on high until smooth and creamy.
3. Enjoy your smoothie.

Nutritional Contents:

- Calories: 266
- Fat: 17g
- Carbohydrates: 7g
- Protein: 22g

Almond and Kale Extreme

Serving: 1

Prep Time: 10 minutes

Ingredients:

- ¼ cup kale, torn
- 2 cups water
- 2-Oz almonds
- 1 packet stevia, if you want
- ½ cup spinach, packed

Directions:

1. Soak almonds in water and keep it overnight.
2. Do not discard water and add all in blender.
3. Add all the listed ingredients to a blender.
4. Blend on high until smooth and creamy.
5. Enjoy your smoothie.

Nutritional Contents:

- Calories: 334
- Fat: 28g
- Carbohydrates: 14g
- Protein: 12g

Healthy Chocolate Milkshake

Serving: 2

Prep Time: 10 minutes

Ingredients:

- 16 ounces unsweetened almond milk, vanilla
- 1 pack stevia
- 1 Scoop Whey isolate chocolate protein powder
- ½ cup crushed ice

Directions:

1. Add listed ingredients to blender
2. Blend until you have a smooth and creamy texture
3. Serve chilled and enjoy!

Nutritional Contents:

- Calories: 292
- Fat: 25g
- Carbohydrates: 4g
- Protein: 15g

Lovely Chocolate Coconut Delight

Serving: 1

Prep Time: 10 minutes

Ingredients:

- 2 tablespoons chocolate powder, unsweetened
- 2 cups water
- 1 ounce pecans
- 1-2 packets Stevia, optional
- 1 tablespoon avocado oil
- 2 tablespoons coconut flakes shredded and unsweetened

Directions:

1. Add all the listed ingredients to a blender.
2. Blend on high until smooth and creamy.
3. Enjoy your smoothie.

Nutritional Contents:

- Calories: 408
- Fat: 38g
- Carbohydrates: 17g
- Protein: 4.9g

The Vegetable Mix

Serving: 2

Prep Time: 10 minutes

Ingredients:

- 1 cup broccoli, steamed
- 1 bunch asparagus, steamed
- 2 cups coconut milk
- 2 tablespoons coconut oil
- 2 carrots, peeled
- Few inch horseradish
- Himalayan salt
- Pinch of chili powder
- ½ a onion
- 2 garlic cloves

Directions:

1. Add all the listed ingredients to your blender except coconut oil, salt and chili powder

2. Blend until smooth

3. Add salt, coconut oil and chili powder

4. Stir well and serve chilled!

Nutritional Contents:

- Calories: 200
- Fat: 12g

- Carbohydrates: 10g
- Protein: 16g

The Berry-Licious And Hazelnut Smoothie

Serving: 1

Prep Time: 10 minutes

Ingredients:

- 1 tablespoon MCT oil
- 2 cups cold water
- 3 large blackberries, whole
- 1-2 packets Stevia, optional
- 2 tablespoons chocolate powder, unsweetened
- 3 tablespoons Hazelnut, chopped
- 1 tablespoon heavy cream

Directions:

1. Add all the listed ingredients to a blender.
2. Blend on high until smooth and creamy.
3. Enjoy your smoothie.

Nutritional Contents:

- Calories: 365
- Fat: 34g
- Carbohydrates: 167g
- Protein: 7g

Pumpkin Pie Buttered Coffee

Serving: 1

Prep Time: 10 minutes

Ingredients:

- 12 ounces hot coffee
- 2 tablespoons canned pumpkin
- 1 tablespoon regular butter, unsalted
- ¼ teaspoon pumpkin pie spice
- Liquid stevia, to sweeten

Directions:

1. Add listed ingredients to blender
2. Blend until you have a smooth and creamy texture
3. Serve chilled and enjoy!

Nutritional Contents:

- Calories: 120
- Fat: 12g
- Carbohydrates: 2g
- Protein: 1g

Peanut Butter Cool Milkshake

Serving: 1

Prep Time: 10 minutes

Ingredients:

- ½ cup coconut milk, regular
- 1 cup unsweetened almond milk, vanilla
- 2 tablespoons all natural peanut butter
- 1 teaspoon vanilla extract

Directions:

1. Add all the listed ingredients to a blender.
2. Blend on high until smooth and creamy.
3. Enjoy your smoothie.

Nutritional Contents:

- Calories: 253
- Fat: 23g
- Carbohydrates: 7g
- Protein: 5g

Cabbage and Chia Glass

Serving: 2

Prep Time: 10 minutes

Ingredients:

- 1/3 cup cabbage
- 1 cup cold unsweetened coconut milk
- 1 tablespoon chia seeds
- ½ cup cherries
- ½ cup spinach

Directions:

1. Add coconut milk to your blender
2. Cut cabbage and add to your blender
3. Place chia seeds in a coffee grinder and chop to powder, brush the powder into blender
4. Pit the cherries and add them to the blender
5. Wash and dry the spinach and chop
6. Add to the mix
7. Cover and blend on low followed by medium
8. Taste the texture and serve chilled!

Nutritional Contents:

- Calories: 181
- Fat: 15g
- Carbohydrates: 8g

- Protein: 5g

The Brazilian Nut Shake

Serving: 1

Prep Time: 10 minutes

Ingredients:

- 1 tablespoon sunflower seeds
- 1 cup water
- 1 ounce Brazil nuts
- 1 tablespoon stevia
- 1 tablespoon MCT oil
- 1 cup Spring mix salad blend

Directions:

1. Add listed ingredients to blender
2. Blend until you have a smooth and creamy texture
3. Serve chilled and enjoy!

Nutritional Contents:

- Calories: 350
- Fat: 36g
- Carbohydrates: 7g
- Protein: 3g

A Winter Smoothie

Serving: 2

Prep Time: 10 minutes

Ingredients:

- 3 tomatoes, peeled
- 1 celery stalk
- 2 cloves garlic, peeled
- 1 inch ginger, peeled
- 1 cucumber, peeled
- Juice of 1 lemon
- 1 cup alkaline water
- Salt as needed
- Pepper as needed
- Pinch of turmeric
- Olive oil/avocado oil

Directions:

1. Add tomatoes, celery, garlic, cucumber and water to your blender
2. Blend well until smooth
3. Add lemon juice, salt and oil
4. Stir
5. Season with pepper and turmeric
6. Stir

7. Serve chilled and enjoy!

Nutritional Contents:

- Calories: 281
- Fat: 25g
- Carbohydrates: 8g
- Protein: 9g

Hardcore Kale Shake

Serving: 1

Prep Time: 10 minutes

Ingredients:

- 1 small sweet potato, cooked, cooled and sliced
- ¾ cup unsweetened almond milk, vanilla
- ½ teaspoon ground cinnamon
- ¼ teaspoon ground nutmeg
- 1 teaspoon pure vanilla extract
- 2 slices avocado, peeled, pitted and sliced
- Liquid stevia
- 1 scoop protein powder

Directions:

1. Add listed ingredients to blender
2. Blend until you have a smooth and creamy texture
3. Serve chilled and enjoy!

Nutritional Contents:

- Calories: 164
- Fat: 11g
- Carbohydrates: 10g
- Protein: 3g

Fine and Smooth Creamy Strawberry Delight

Serving: 1

Prep Time: 10 minutes

Ingredients:

- 1 cup ice cubes
- ½ cup water
- 1 scoop strawberry whey protein powder
- 3 slices avocado, peeled and pitted
- 1 ounce MCT oil
- ½ cup frozen strawberries, unsweetened

Directions:

1. Add listed ingredients to blender
2. Blend until you have a smooth and creamy texture
3. Serve chilled and enjoy!

Nutritional Contents:

- Calories: 133
- Fat: 39g
- Carbohydrates: 10g
- Protein: 27g

CONCLUSION

I can't express how honored I am to think that you found my book interesting and informative enough to read it all through to the end.

I thank you again for purchasing this book and I hope that you had as much fun reading it as I had writing it.

I bid you farewell and encourage you to move forward with your Keto Smoothie journey!

38483301R00054

Printed in Poland
by Amazon Fulfillment
Poland Sp. z o.o., Wrocław